HOW THEY LIVED

A CAVALRY CORPORAL

JAY SCHLEIFER

Illustrated by
Jerry Harston

ROURKE BOOK COMPANY, INC.
Vero Beach, Florida 32964

Text © 1994 Rourke Book Company, Inc.
P.O. Box 3328, Vero Beach, Florida 32964

All rights reserved. No part of this book may be reproduced or utilized in any form or by any means, electronic or mechanical including photocopying, recording, or by any information storage and retrieval system without permission in writing from the publisher.

A Blackbirch Graphics Book.

Printed in the United States of America.

Library of Congress Cataloging-in-Publication Data

Schleifer, Jay.
    A cavalry corporal / by Jay Schleifer; illustrated by Jerry Harston.
      p.   cm. — (How they lived)
  ISBN 1-55916-043-8
    1. West (U.S)—History—1860–1890—Juvenile literature. 2. United States. Army. Cavalry—History—19th century—Juvenile literature. 3. United States. Army—Military life—History—19th century—Juvenile literature. 4. Indians of North America—Wars—1866–1895—Juvenile literature. 5. Frontier and pioneer life—West (U.S.)—Juvenile literature. 6. Soldiers—West (U.S.)—History—19th century—Juvenile literature. I. Title. II. Series: How they lived (Vero Beach, Fla.)
F594.S36   1994
978'.02—dc20
                                                      94-1781
                                                          CIP

Printed in the USA   AC

CONTENTS

THE LONG RIDE 4

◆

THE HORSE SOLDIERS 6

◆

WESTERN LANDSCAPE 8

◆

FORTS ACROSS THE FRONTIER 10

◆

UNIFORMS AND WEAPONS 12

◆

HORSES 14

◆

BARRACKS LIFE 16

◆

MEDICINE AND HEALTH 18

◆

DISCIPLINE IN THE RANKS 20

◆

THE OFFICERS 22

◆

WHY DID THEY FIGHT? 24

◆

THE CAMPAIGN TRAIL 26

◆

CUSTER'S LAST STAND 28

◆

THE LAST CAVALRY CHARGE 30

◆

GLOSSARY 31

◆

INDEX 32

THE LONG RIDE

The young cavalry corporal pulled his buffalo-skin coat tightly against his body, trying to keep out the biting wind of a very cold winter morning. Gently, he urged his horse on through the foot-deep snow.

Often, a cavalry soldier would march for many days through the wild American West. During the winter, soldiers suffered extreme cold and fatigue as they traveled. Food supplies consisted of salt pork and coffee. These supplies had to last for a long time, as a soldier's destination could be miles away.

A cavalry soldier would have 200 other troopers from the U.S. Cavalry with him. Cavalry soldiers rode in groups of four. If attacked, three men in each group would grab their rifles and fight, while the fourth held the horses.

There was always a chance of being attacked, because the cavalry often rode near Native American villages. Sometimes, the cavalry made the first move and charged a Native American village. Because settlers had often complained that Native Americans had attacked their ranches, it became the cavalry's job to protect the settlers.

Native Americans fought to protect their lands from being taken by newcomers from the East. Many of the settlers killed buffalo for sport and trampled the Native Americans' sacred places.

When a cavalry unit sighted a village, officers issued orders. Then, a bugler sounded the charge. Some troopers might have felt it was wrong to attack people in a sleeping village. However, it was their duty; and doing one's duty was at the heart of being a cavalry soldier.

Sleeping Native Americans were often attacked by cavalry soldiers who were under orders to protect frontier settlers.

THE HORSE SOLDIERS

There have been horse-mounted soldiers as long as there have been armies. The Asian, Egyptian, and Roman nations all used cavalry troops. The knights of Old England were troopers who rode into battle, covered with heavy armor.

The power of the cavalry came from how it shocked its enemy with speed and surprise. Unlike slow-moving foot soldiers, troops on horse-back could attack an enemy suddenly. Then, they could disappear before the enemy knew fully what had hit them.

European wars often included great charges of thousands of cavalry. When European military leaders moved to America, they formed a cavalry corps (a unit of military service) to fight the British in the Revolutionary War. However, there was little room in the thick forests for such a large number of horse-mounted soldiers.

Later wars were fought in more open spaces. The cavalry attacked bravely during the Mexican War of the 1840s, and then had a major role in the Civil War. Great forces of cavalry, often called dragoons, ranged across the battlegrounds of North and South. They attacked supplies, and broke up the enemy's ability to fight as a unit. One of the most famous troops was led by General J.E.B. Stuart of the South.

Another role also made the cavalry famous—their part in the shaping of the American West. In the 1830s, pioneers began to move in great numbers from the eastern forests into more open lands. This was the homeland of many Native American tribes. Settlers often reported that the Native Americans were among the best riders they had ever seen.

Settlers were often victims of attacks by certain Native American tribes, and did not have enough horses to be able to fight back or escape. These pioneers sent out a call for help and horse protection from the army. The cavalry then began its sixty-year-long western ride.

English knights and their horses dressed in heavy armor.

Early American soldiers dressed in the much lighter uniform of their units.

Western Landscape

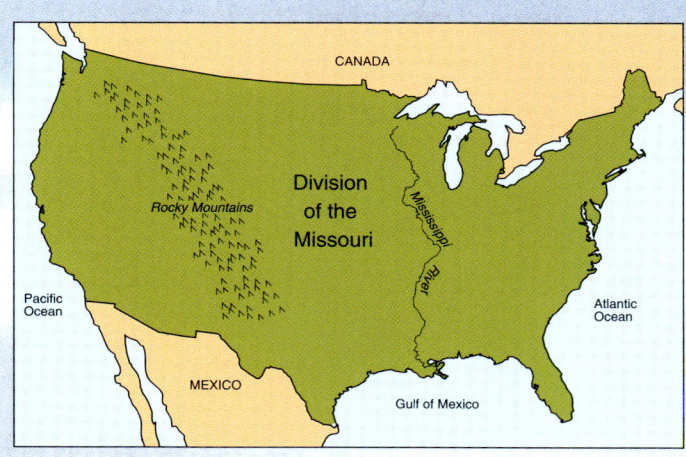

Many U.S. Cavalry units fought, lived, and died on a giant battlefield that stretched across two thirds of the American continent. Called the "Division of the Missouri," this territory included more than 2 million square miles and stretched from the Mississippi River in the East to the Rocky Mountains in the West, and from Canada to Mexico.

While patrolling the Division, troopers would be challenged by an incredible variety of landscapes and climates. There were broad grasslands where days of riding barely changed the view, and where unbelievable herds of buffalo made the earth shake with their passing. In the southwestern deserts, temperatures often rose to 110 degrees Fahrenheit, while the dust kicked up by the horses choked man and beast at every step. Watering holes were usually days apart. Then, when water was finally found, it was sometimes undrinkable.

In the North, cavalry units would climb through twisted canyons and steeply forested mountain passes that were often thousands of feet high. A single misstep by a soldier or horse could mean a deadly fall.

Though the summers were fierce, the winters could be much worse. Blizzards were common, with six-foot snowdrifts and winds that raced at the speed of present-day automobiles. Spring brought milder weather, but melted snow swelled the rivers. A flash flood could carry away a soldier in seconds if he was unlucky enough to be riding his horse through a riverbed when the river swelled.

Snakes, scorpions, wolves, and poisonous plants were also dangers in the lives of cavalry soldiers.

All of these severe hardships had negative effects on the cavalry troops. Physically, they were often miserable. However, they managed to find strength in each other and beauty in the wild land. They could even make jokes about their surroundings. One soldier reported the proper way to drink water: "Take a mouthful, squeeze out the mud with your teeth, swallow the rest!"

Opposite: Some cavalry soldiers had to patrol large areas of land during terrible snowstorms.

FORTS ACROSS THE FRONTIER

Some frontier forts were constructed with high fences for protection from attacks.

Cavalry troopers spent about half their time on the trail. The rest of the year, they were housed in their forts. The largest forts were sturdy buildings with high fences for protection. More commonly, though, forts were thrown together with whatever materials could be found. One type of material was adobe, a kind of dried mud that could melt during the rainy season and fall on a soldier's head.

Forts were always built near water and grasslands where the horses could feed. The buildings usually included officers' quarters, storehouses, stables, and barracks for the troopers. Life was rough at best. One officer visited a typical barracks and described it as "too small, poorly built, usually overcrowded, drafty, too cold in winter, and too hot in summer."

Officers lived better than the soldiers. Even in the worst locations, they would have their own houses, with two to four rooms. Some even had neatly tended gardens.

Sergeants and corporals, called non-commissioned officers by the army, slept with the troopers. However, their rank brought them the best bunks in the barracks—the ones near the windows in summer, closest to the heat stove in the winter.

The best fort to serve in was probably Fort Riley, Kansas, where a comfortable mess hall served 2,000 troopers at a time. The worst was Fort Ruby on the Utah-Nevada border. It had no comforts of any kind. The soldiers hated it so much they offered to trade the government $30,000 in back pay it owed them for orders out. Fort Ruby's commanding officer's first order was to award himself a six-month vacation!

Cavalry horses could drink from the lakes or streams that were near a fort.

Uniforms and Weapons

The basic uniform of the cavalry trooper was like that of the army's foot soldiers. However, troopers would always add something special to it. Often, it was a pair of spit-shined, high leather riding boots, complete with spurs, and a cowboy style gunbelt.

On duty, troopers wore small flat-top hats. On the trail, they would switch to a campaign hat, somewhat like those the cowboys wore. Its broad brim helped protect their eyes from the baking sun. Such hats sometimes became drinking bowls as well.

Officers often inspected the uniforms of their troops for neatness.

Officers were easy to spot by their brass buttons and gold-colored shoulder bars. Many officers also wore a colored stripe on their pant legs. On parade, they would wear helmets decorated with feathers or even buffalo hair.

Uniforms carried markings that showed a soldier's rank and job. The markings were of different colors for different parts of the army. The infantry wore white, the medical corps green, the artillery red. The cavalry proudly wore gold!

Winter wear included long buffalo-skin coats, muskrat hats, and sometimes woolen face masks. Though the winter clothing was effective, some troopers wore layers of their own clothes underneath for added warmth.

The cavalry got some of the army's best weapons. Troopers carried rifles that were shorter and lighter than the regular rifles others carried. Some were issued Colt 45 six-shooter revolvers. The Colt 45 has been called "the gun that won the West."

Troopers also were given some of the service's least usable weapons. They carried

Cavalry troopers were issued rifles, or guns, and swords to protect themselves in battle.

sabers—curved battle swords. The swords looked very dangerous, but could not protect the cavalry against long distance weapons such as rifles or arrows. They also received the Gatling gun, a hand-cranked machine gun. A Gatling had up to 10 barrels that revolved, so some could be reloaded while the others fired. The gun was said to fire 400 shots a minute, but it often didn't work. Gatlings often overheated after just a few shots.

HORSES

Cavalry horses were usually bought from local ranchers or brought in from other forts. They were not like the warhorses raised and ridden by the Native American tribes, but were ordinary workhorses. They would be delivered untrained, often in large numbers.

The first task that needed to be done was called breaking-in—getting an animal used to the feeling of a bridle and saddle, and then to the weight of a rider on its back.

The first challenge was to get an animal saddled. To do this, specially trained troopers would shove a horse on its side, hold it down as it kicked and brayed, and place a blindfold on it. Finally, a saddle was strapped in place, and a horse would be allowed to rise and walk around.

After a horse could stand a saddle, a rider would add his weight and the war between man and beast would begin. Riders hung on while horses kicked, bucked, shook, and tried to throw them off. More than one trooper ended up on the hard ground, his mouth full of dirt, hearing what sounded like a loud horse-laugh above him. However, in time, each animal would learn the first lesson of life in the

14

army—to take all orders from those above.

Once trained, each horse was paired with a rider and the two often became attached. It was a tragedy when either was lost in battle. "I found Sam shot in the belly," one trooper reported of his mount, "so I turned him loose to go off and die. But he followed me like a dog, pushing his head against me and groaning like a person. I had to shoot him to end his misery. He was a splendid horse!"

Soldiers broke in untrained horses in order to be able to ride them.

Barracks Life

Most cavalry troopers signed on for five-year terms in the service, with about half that time spent in forts. Each day would have its own routine, and the sound of the bugle set the routine.

The first time it sounded was at 5:30 A.M., waking the post, or fort. By 6:15 A.M., the bugle was calling the troopers to drill. Work periods, called fatigues, were held at 7:30 A.M. and 1:00 P.M. Tasks included cooking, cleaning, cutting wood, and doing construction work. There would be another drill period at 4:30 P.M. Then, the playing of "Taps" at 8:15 P.M. signaled the end of the official day.

Guard mount was held each morning. This was when men on guard duty were inspected by their officers. The men competed with each other to see who could look the sharpest. The trooper with the blackest boots, neatest creases, or best overall look would be made orderly for the day to the fort's commander. As an orderly, he would carry messages and run errands, but was excused from drills and fatigues—a prize worth winning.

Drills included marching and other military skills, but didn't often include target practice. Bullets were always in short supply, and the lack of training showed. Some troopers had to learn how to use their rifles in battle, and some died trying.

Meals were basic—mostly beans, salt pork, hardtack (a kind of hard bread), bacon, and sometimes buffalo meat. Food often arrived at the fort already rotten. Pay was just $16 per month until 1871, and then it was reduced to $13 per month. Congress cut the army's budget to save money.

Even with all these hardships, many troopers stayed in the service after their first terms were over. Team spirit was often high, and the men developed deep friendships. They often dreamed up their own forms of fun. Some men played the banjo or harmonica while others sang along. Barracks card games went on for hours.

For entertainment in the barracks, soldiers often played instruments and sang songs.

Medicine and Health

Troopers feared the guns and arrows of the enemy, and often had wounds that needed medical treatment. During the 1800s, medical care was not as advanced as it is today.

The army doctors were called surgeons. Often, many doctors had formal medical educations, but they faced a lack of proper supplies.

Whether the problem was frostbite or an infection from an open wound, doctors often felt that an operation was the only answer. Amputation—the removal of an injured limb—was one of the most common operations. For this reason, surgeons carried a kit that contained forty-seven instruments, most of which were designed to cut into the body.

The kit included a foot-long saw made to cut bone. There was also a set of long needles (one nearly eighteen inches in length) used to drill into areas filled with blood, to help it drain out of the body. There were clamps for holding the skin open or closed, and a set of sewing needles for patching wounds.

Painkillers, however, were not in the kit. Patients were put to sleep by being made to drink alcohol, or were simply held down firmly while the doctors operated. Germ killers were not usually available either. When an operation did not kill a man, the infections that often occurred afterward could.

A serious injury to the stomach or head usually meant death for a trooper. Most army surgeons had not been trained to handle such difficult wounds. However, a trooper might survive an arm or leg injury. Even if he lost the limb, his life would be saved. On average, only half of all wounded soldiers lived through their injuries.

Disease was also a health problem for the soldier. Rotten food, poor living conditions (few forts had bathhouses), and a lack of health knowledge, made forts breeding grounds for germs. There was little the army doctors could do except to advise the men to stay as clean as possible.

Opposite: Army doctors often had to perform surgery on cavalry soldiers who were wounded in battle.

Discipline in the Ranks

The cavalry units were governed by many laws and rules. The rulebook that the army used was extremely thick, and punishments for breaking any of the cavalry rules could be very harsh.

Minor crimes included fighting, drunkenness, or petty theft. It was a much more serious crime to fall asleep while on guard duty, refuse an order, or strike an officer. Most common among the serious crimes committed by a soldier was desertion—running away from the army.

Most soldiers accused of crimes received a trial, called a court-martial. There were an incredible number of these trials. At one fort, there were only 3,008 soldiers on the post, but over 2,000 court-martials were held!

The officer serving as the judge at the trial would often sentence a trooper to a pay loss, hard labor, or time in the guardhouse—the army's version of jail. Often, some tough commanders would make these punishments even harder. The guardhouse at one post was a fifteen-foot-deep hole in the ground. Hard labor would sometimes mean marching with a heavy log until the trooper dropped from exhaustion. Deserters would have a heavy iron ball and chain attached to their legs to make sure they would not run away again.

There were also several different types of illegal punishments. Some troopers were hung by their thumbs or wrists. In other instances, two men who had argued were ordered to beat each other with bullwhips. For at least twelve crimes, the army rulebook allowed the death penalty.

Opposite: Some cavalry troopers who broke army rules were placed in a guardhouse as punishment.

THE OFFICERS

Life at a cavalry fort was different for officers and troopers. Ordinary troopers lived in a world of crowded barracks, poor pay, and few comforts. Officers, however, lived in their own houses, often with their wives and children. They ate better food, rode finer horses, and ordered hard work to be done instead of doing it themselves. Officers were more able to get away with crimes, like drunkenness, for which troopers would be punished.

The officer's world was closed to regular troopers—"off limits"—was the army term. Still, some officers refused to accept any special favors. General Phillip Sheridan, commander of the entire Division of the Missouri, was known for living as his troops did, even sleeping in tents with them in the rain. Other officers, such as General George Custer, made a show of their fancy uniforms and privileges.

As an officer, General George Custer had more privileges than regular army soldiers.

Officers would ride in front of their men while out on patrol.

However, it was usually the lieutenants, the lowest class of officers, who made the most fuss about their rank, refusing even to talk to the troopers. Any message from an officer to a trooper never went directly to him but would be sent by a sergeant to a corporal, who would finally give it to a private.

Troopers often complained about the special favors officers received. Yet they also remembered that, on the trail, most officers really looked out for their men. Usually it was the officers who rode right up front, ahead of their men, making themselves the first and easiest targets to attackers.

WHY DID THEY FIGHT?

The late 1800s were a sad time in the West. Two great peoples—Native Americans and American pioneers—often made war on each other. There are many reasons why the white settlers and Native Americans fought, but one of the most important reasons was the lack of understanding of each other's culture.

The settlers fought because they felt God meant the land to be theirs. Originally, many

had come from other lands and had helped to settle the eastern coast of the United States.

Now the settlers felt it was their fate to control all the land between the East and West coasts. They wanted to farm, mine, and build factories, cities, roads, and railways. To the settlers, Native American tribes were an uneducated, savage people who just happened to be on the land. They felt it was necessary and right to remove them from it.

Native Americans saw an opposite picture: The land, the lakes, and the buffalo were gifts of nature that had provided for their peoples for many generations. Native American tribes were willing to share with the newcomers, but the settlers wanted it all. They fenced in lands that the Native Americans had ridden openly. The settlers were mean, dishonest, and a threat to the Native Americans' very survival.

Once violence broke out, both sides were very cruel. Native Americans knew the country well, and fought with daring and bravery. The newcomers, though, had better weapons and supplies, which never seemed to run out. They also had a trained army to fight for them—the U.S. Cavalry.

In the end, it was just a matter of time until the cavalry won the war.

Native Americans and the cavalry frequently fought over land.

THE CAMPAIGN TRAIL

Once war broke out, the cavalry realized the only way to clear an area of warring tribes was to go out after them. Cavalry troops rode out of the forts in long lines, from a few dozen troopers to more than a thousand. Officers led the way and supply wagons brought up the rear. The rides, called campaigns, could last from a few days to several months.

Along with his rifle, each man carried a 50 pound pack. It held clothes, a blanket and sheets, half of a two-man tent, food, and 150 bullets. Each man also carried 15 pounds of grain for his horse.

Troopers would march for half the day, then would eat and rest. When the enemy was near, however, they would be on the move for twenty-four hours or more, rain or shine.

The Native Americans were skilled at moving silently, then attacking suddenly. Warwhoops, gunfire, and arrows could come at any time, and from any

direction. Often, by the time the troopers were ready to return the fire, the fast-moving warriors were gone.

Approximately 200,000 Native Americans lived in the Division of the Missouri. Yet only about 15,000 troopers rode against them. The numbers, though, did not tell the full story. Many of the Native Americans were children and others who were too weak to fight.

At times, some battles led to peace agreements. Native Americans were promised that if they gave up certain lands, other lands would be theirs to keep. Often, settlers broke these promises, and new battles broke out.

At first, most battles were fought during the warmer months. Then, the cavalry began to attack in the winter, when the tribes were at rest in their villages. The results were horrible for the tribes. Those not killed, were forced into the cold. Their only choices were to surrender or freeze. In the end, many surrendered.

Troopers on the campaign trail were often on the lookout for Native American warriors.

27

Custer's Last Stand

The U.S. Cavalry may best be remembered for a battle it lost. The officer who was defeated was George Armstrong Custer.

General Custer was one of the army's best known cavalry officers—a Civil War hero who had been made a commander at age twenty-three.

In the summer of 1876, Custer led 600 troopers toward a river called the Little Bighorn in what is now Montana. Scouts had brought word of a gigantic Native American gathering in the area. Some 15,000 Sioux, Cheyenne, and other tribes had come together under a powerful chief named Sitting Bull. The U.S. government had promised the tribes that the Black Hills, a sacred area in present-day South Dakota, would always be theirs. However, gold had been found in the Black Hills and settlers poured into the area. The Native American tribal leaders needed to decide what to do.

General Custer and his troops were outnumbered by Native Americans protecting their land during the Battle of Little Bighorn.

Although he was far outnumbered, Custer ordered an attack. Splitting his cavalry troops in three parts, Custer rode into the valley of the Little Bighorn. At first the attack went well. Suddenly, a group of several hundred cavalry

soldiers were surrounded by a force of 2,000 warriors.

Dismounted from their horses and formed into a circle, the troopers fought desperately. However, every last one of this group died, many horribly. The other two cavalry groups escaped to tell the tale.

Some newspapers reported the truth, but many others declared it was the Native American tribes, not Custer, who attacked. Readers demanded revenge. Thousands of new cavalry poured into the area, forcing Sitting Bull to flee to Canada. Custer's Last Stand, as the battle was called, became another reason to force Native Americans from lands that had been promised to them.

The Last Cavalry Charge

By 1900, the battles in the West were over. Many Native American tribes had given up their homelands and been moved into special areas called reservations. With the West settled, it seemed that the cavalry was no longer needed.

However, the cavalry had one more battle to win. Since the days of Columbus, Spain had ruled Cuba. In the mid-1890s, the Cuban people began a fight for freedom. The U.S. government rushed to their aid. The conflict that resulted was called the Spanish-American War.

When the war began, volunteers were asked to fight in Cuba. A young man named Theodore Roosevelt answered.

The Rough Riders charged San Juan Hill during the U.S. war against Spain.

Teddy Roosevelt had spent years working on western ranches. He put out a call for people to join his troop, and hundreds responded. They formed the First Volunteer Cavalry, nicknamed "Roosevelt's Rough Riders."

In 1898, the Rough Riders left for Cuba. Strangely, this new cavalry unit left its horses at home. There just wasn't room for the horses on the ships. Only Roosevelt brought his mount.

In Cuba, the Rough Riders showed they could fight just as well on foot as on horseback. With Roosevelt leading the charge, they stormed San Juan Hill, an important Spanish post, and helped U.S. troops win the war in just four months. The Rough Riders' fame spread far and wide and Teddy Roosevelt went on to be elected president in 1904.

The Rough Riders included several Native Americans. A few years before, they might have fought against the cavalry, not as a part of it. An overseas war had brought Americans of all races together.

Glossary

adobe Dried mud or clay used for building walls or roofing.

amputation Removal of an arm, leg, finger, or toe.

breaking-in The process of training a horse to accept a saddle and a rider.

campaign A mission or ride of the cavalry.

cavalry Mounted soldiers.

court-martial A trial held by the army.

desertion Unlawfully leaving the army.

dragoons European term for cavalry troops.

fatigues Work periods on an army base.

Gatling gun A fast-firing machine gun.

guard mount The daily inspection of cavalry troops assigned to guard duty by their officers.

hardtack A hard, baked bread.

infantry Foot soldiers.

off limits Term meaning entry is against the rules.

reservation Parcels of land set aside for Native Americans by the U.S. government.

saber A curved sword carried by cavalry troops.

Index

American West, 4, 6, 24, 30

Black Hills, 28

Campaign trails, 26–27
Civil War, 6, 28
Colt 45, 13
Court-martial, 20
Custer, George, 22, 28
Custer's Last Stand, 28–29

Discipline, 20
Division of the Missouri, 9, 22, 27
Dragoons, 6
Drills, 17

Fatigues, 16, 17
Foot soldiers, 6, 12
Fort Riley, 11
Fort Ruby, 11
Forts, 10–11, 26

Gatling gun, 13
Guard mount, 17

Horse soldiers (history of), 6
Horses, 14–15

Little Bighorn, 28

Medical care, 18–19
Mexican War, 6
Mississippi River, 9

Native Americans, 5, 6, 14, 24, 25–26, 28
Non-commissioned officers, 11

Officers, 5, 22–23
   quarters of, 10
   uniforms of, 10
Off limits, 22

Revolutionary War, 6
Rocky Moutains, 9
Roosevelt, Theodore, 30
Roosevelt's Rough Riders, 30

Sabers, 13
Settlers, 5, 6, 24–25
Sheridan, Phillip, 22
Sitting Bull, 28, 29
Spanish-American War, 30
Stuart, J.E.B., 6
Surgeons, 19

Troopers
   barracks of, 10, 16–17
   entertainment of, 17
   landscape and, 9
   meals of, 17
   pay of, 17
   service of, 16
   supplies of, 4, 26
   uniforms of, 12–13

Acknowledgments and Photo Credits
Cover by Gene Biggs. Interior artwork by Jerry Harston.
Pages 13, 22, 23, 24, 30: North Wind Picture Archives.